Original title:
Crickets, Frogs, and Couplets

Copyright © 2025 Creative Arts Management OÜ
All rights reserved.

Author: Helena Marchant
ISBN HARDBACK: 978-1-80567-447-4
ISBN PAPERBACK: 978-1-80567-746-8

Nighttime's Resonance

In the dark, they hold their cheer,
Bouncing tunes for all to hear.
With legs so long, and voices loud,
They sing their songs, oh how they're proud.

Hopping here and leaping there,
Oh, what a joyful, quirky fare.
With every chirp, they tell their tales,
Of daring dreams and epic trails.

Beneath the moon, they dance and play,
Creating rhythms in a silly way.
While shadows sway and eavesdroppers peek,
In the night, their laughter's unique.

Whimsical whispers, a funny treat,
On wobbly feet, they stomp the beat.
As stars above begin to glint,
They frolic on, with cheeky hints.

Secret Serenades

In the cool breeze, giggles flop,
As tiny legs take a happy hop.
With every note, they squeeze out glee,
Making melodies, wild and free.

Behind the leaves, mischief blooms,
A symphony of tiny booms.
In harmony, they take their stand,
Creating chaos in the land.

A splash of sound, a sudden squawk,
They serenade the midnight block.
Fingers tap on bark and stone,
In their secret club, they're never alone.

With quirky tunes that twist and turn,
In surprising rhythms, they all yearn.
Under silver beams, they pull off tricks,
In this wild concert, everyone clicks.

Echo Chamber

In the dark of night, they sing,
With raspy notes that make hearts sting.
A chorus rises, funny and loud,
As shadows dance, forming a crowd.

Underneath the moon's bright gleam,
Creatures croon, living the dream.
They joke about the awkward slips,
And share the tales of tiny trips.

With every chirp, a tale unfolds,
Of secret whispers, laughters bold.
They poke fun at the passing breeze,
In the booming sound of leafy trees.

Mirth in the air, a playful shout,
As echoes linger, dancing about.
Their giggles twirl in the cool night air,
While mischief lurks, without a care.

Nature's Chat

In the garden where night unfolds,
Little voices, funny stories told.
A banter blooms beneath the moon,
With winks and nods, they jest and croon.

One complains of a big old toad,
And how he's known to steal the show.
Another chuckles, 'He's quite absurd,
Always hopping, but rarely heard!'

Quips fly like stars in a night sky,
With each short line, they let out a sigh.
They chuckle at the fields so wide,
Imagining adventures on every ride.

As laughter echoes, a merry tune,
In Nature's chat, beneath the moon.
Their jests linger, carried by the breeze,
Sharing laughter, aiming to please.

Murmurs of the Marsh

In the marsh where mischief brews,
Funny tales hide in the morning hues.
Mumbling whispers and giggles abound,
As laughter dances all around.

One tells of a fish that wore a hat,
While others shriek, "Is that a fact?"
The reeds listen with eager ears,
As tiny feet skip and stretch in cheers.

Each ripple carries a silly joke,
With every jump, they provoke and poke.
Slime on the path seems to be their muse,
As they slip and slide, just to amuse.

Together they weave a wondrous night,
Murmurs of fun in the dim twilight.
With brushes of green and shades of brown,
In their marshy realm, laughs float around.

Soothing Sounds

In the twilight glow, jokes unfold,
With patterns of laughter, stories told.
A symphony swells, soft and sweet,
As punchlines tumble, light on their feet.

With trails of giggles on every beat,
They make the night feel pleasantly complete.
Each sound a note, a chuckle shared,
In harmony, they dance, unprepared.

A tap here, a croak there,
Music of humor fills the air.
As tiny creatures play their part,
With each merry note, they steal the heart.

In soothing sounds, the night thrives,
Amidst the laughs, hilarity dives.
The world around, a lively show,
Crafted with joy, like a dazzling glow.

Nightfall Nocturne

As sun dips low, the giggles start,
Little creatures play their part.
With leaps and bounds, they hop about,
In a silly dance, with a joyful shout.

They sing their tunes from leafy homes,
While stars peek through, like tiny gnomes.
Whispers float on the evening air,
A gathering of laughter everywhere.

Nature's Whispered Words

In the dusky glow, the chorus roars,
Jokes and laughter, behind closed doors.
High-pitched chats and ribbits so clear,
Witty banter, no room for fear.

Tails wagging, their punchlines fly,
Underneath the twinkling sky.
Comedic timing, a lively jest,
In the theater of nature's best.

Dances in the Dark

Underneath the cloak of night,
Tiny dancers show their might.
They twirl and leap with comic flair,
Shining bright, like a fairground fair.

A jig or two, then off they go,
What a sight, what a show!
Spinning tales in the moonlight's glow,
With each leap, their giggles grow.

Farewell to the Day

As daylight bows and shadows creep,
The playful crowd begins to leap.
With no regrets, they start to play,
Cackles rising as night meets day.

In moonlit fields, the antics unfold,
Stories shared that never get old.
With a wink and a chuckle, they lay down,
As twilight arrives, they claim the crown.

Jamboree of the Biography

In the night, a party brews,
With singers dressed in vibrant hues.
They chirp and croak, a lively bunch,
As starlit stars attend the lunch.

Amid the grass, a dance takes flight,
Twisting tails in sheer delight.
The moonlight beams on all that sings,
While critters boast of funny things.

A toad in a waistcoat claims the floor,
His debut dance—what a uproar!
While shadows shimmy, lost in bliss,
Nothing's missed in this silly twist.

From all corners, laughter flows,
As nature's show puts on its prose.
The beat goes on—who needs a band?
When joy can leap with every hand.

Voices of the Underbrush

Down in the thicket, tales emerge,
With creaky voices that sure diverge.
One croaks a joke about a leaf,
While others chime in, beyond belief.

A wanderer shows up with flair,
Says he's won in trivia—no one's aware!
The vines chuckle, a soft refrain,
As laughter echoes, sweet and plain.

A clamorous crew, it's quite a scene,
With antics wild, so carefree and keen.
A wise old bug gives sage advice,
While critters giggle and roll the dice.

As shadows stretch and colors fade,
The hidden jests never do degrade.
In this realm, it's all in jest,
Where every croon is truly blessed.

Hidden Harmonies

A symphony lurks where few can see,
Silly strings plucked by the willow tree.
With every croak, a tune is spun,
As nature orchestrates the fun.

Subtle whispers dance in the air,
As friends jive close without a care.
While moonbeams twirl like chips in a pot,
A serenade forms, bright and hot.

The passion blossoms, oh what a sound,
As beats bounce off the ground all around.
A gathering thrives in secret delight,
With laughter blooming like flowers at night.

In the hush of the dusk, magic's made,
Where every creature's part is played.
From simple notes to joyful cheers,
This hidden realm erases all fears.

Earthbound Elegies

In the realm where feet are loud,
And dreams are lost in every crowd.
They take their seats upon the grass,
With tales to spin—they'll raise a glass!

A fellow near with a twitching grin,
Sings of rivals who almost win.
With every stanza, they burst with pride,
As nature hums in sync beside.

Lamenting lost socks, dreams fused tight,
While grasshoppers leap, a grand delight.
Imagined trophies adorn each head,
As giggles linger where hopes are fed.

The night is young, the scrapes stand tall,
And through it all, they'll laugh or fall.
A dance with fate, so plucky and bright,
These earthbound dreams sparkle with light.

Resonance of the Dusk

The little jumpers sing their tunes,
Beneath the pale glow of the moon.
A night of chatter, hops, and whirs,
Where silliness dances, none deter ours.

With tiny legs and vast delight,
They chirp and leap into the night.
A tangle of sounds that tickle the air,
Creating a mess of a cheerful affair.

Amid the grass, the laughter spills,
As antics lead to noisy thrills.
A concert grand, yet awkward too,
What will they do? Oh, who knew?

So gather round, join the feast,
Where the merry makers never cease.
In the twilight, a jolly crowd,
Echoes of fun, and we're feeling proud.

Lullabies in Green

In the patch of leaves, a ruckus unfolds,
With chuckles and banter, the story is told.
They hop and wiggle, in playful disguise,
While shadows embrace under starlit skies.

A laughing contest, who can be loud?
The champions of ribbits, a cheeky crowd.
One plops too hard, with a splash and a grin,
While others just giggle, their excitement a sin.

In a world of wiggles, they don't lose the beat,
As rhythm and laughter craft the night sweet.
It's a raucous ballet, a comical scene,
Where every twist brings joy unforeseen.

So join in the frolic, let your heart cheer,
For where there's fun, there's nothing to fear.
With crummy tunes and a dash of glee,
Together we'll dance, wild and free!

Symphony of the Wild

A cacophony rises, the night comes alive,
With giggles and croaks, as all creatures strive.
Their chorus a melody, a flagrant affair,
Where silliness reigns from here to there.

They leap in the air, then tumble about,
In moments of chaos, laughter's what sprout.
With a hop and a skip, they steal the night's stage,
Creating a ruckus that never grows age.

The jester brigade of the grassy expanse,
Shoulder to shoulder, they jiggle and prance.
As glittering stars sprinkle the dome,
They revel in antics, forever at home.

So step into this world, embrace the delight,
Where humor and joy make everything bright.
Each leap is a laugh, every sound is a cheer,
In the wild's orchestra, you'll find your good cheer!

Evocative Echoes

As dusk turns the sky into a playful stage,
A quirky parade is all the rage.
With raspy voices, they share their glee,
Echoes of antics, a comic spree.

Clusters of laughter, mischief in tow,
Leapfrogging friends in a giggly flow.
One takes a plunge, a splat in the pond,
While others erupt in a cackle so fond.

From leafy perch to slippery slopes,
They weave through the night, tangled in hopes.
Every croak a punchline, oh what a jest,
In the landscape of laughter, we're truly blessed.

As echoes linger on this whimsical night,
Join in the revelry, let spirits take flight.
For amid the chuckles, the night is alive,
In the heart of the wild, we laugh and thrive.

Springtime Rhapsody

In the grass, a little jig,
A bounce and croak, oh what a gig!
Tiny singers, making cheer,
As bugs do dance, the season's here.

A ribbit here, a chirp delight,
They prance about in moon's soft light.
Jumping high, with glee they play,
In the green, it's a wild ballet.

A spotlight shines on all their moves,
In nature's stage, each one improves.
With legs that leap and voices strong,
Their laughter weaves a joyful song.

So grab your friends, and let's all cheer,
For nature's jesters, ever near!
With squeaks and hops, they take the scene,
In springtime's joy, we reign supreme.

Hymns of the Wetlands

In puddles deep, the fun begins,
With splashes loud and silly grins.
Notes of laughter, sing along,
In this wetland, we can't go wrong.

The mossy stage, a slippery spot,
Where dancers twirl, give all they've got.
Around the reeds, they swirl and dart,
Creating chaos with every part.

To rhythmic croaks and playful roars,
They laugh and leap from shores to shores.
No dull moment here at all,
In wetlands, joy stands proud and tall.

So raise a cheer for every jest,
These merry souls, they are the best!
With every splash, they fill the air,
In harmony, without a care.

Sounds of the Stillness

In the quiet night, a noise that thrills,
With subtle sounds that dance on hills.
A symphony, so odd and grand,
Nature's quirks, all unplanned.

The darkness hums with cheeky glee,
As echoes bounce from tree to tree.
In hushed tones, they find their way,
A comic show that needs no play.

With starlit skies as their backdrop,
They twirl and jig—oh never stop!
The stillness breaks with giggles loud,
In shadowed corners, laughter's proud.

So listen close to nature's song,
In a world where sillies belong!
Each croak and croon a spark of fun,
Under the moon, the night's not done!

The Enchanted Evening

As twilight creeps, begins the cheer,
With frolicsome tunes that fill the sphere.
Little jesters in the glow,
They twist and turn, put on a show.

In golden light, they leap and laugh,
Performing for a curious staff.
The stars above twinkle in delight,
Encouraging leaps in the night.

Beneath the boughs, a whimsical feast,
As silly antics never cease.
With laughter bright, they claim the scene,
What a magical, funny routine!

So gather 'round for one more tune,
As nature croons beneath the moon.
An enchanted evening's joyful spark,
Where every creature leaves a mark.

Chorus of Dusk and Dew

As the sun dips low with a wink,
Tiny friends begin to clink.
A symphony of silly sounds,
Funny leaps from grassy mounds.

With a chirp and a croak, oh so bright,
Who knew the night could bring such light?
They dance and mingle without care,
In this wild and joyful air.

A lizard pops out with a grin,
Joining in with a silly spin.
The moon laughs down, just a bit,
At all this fun, it can't quite sit.

With a twirl and a hop, the show unfolds,
In the cool of night, the story molds.
The giggles rise, then start to mingle,
Like an orchestra playing a cheeky jingle.

Nature's Harmony in the Shadows

Underneath the starry dome,
Voices rise, a funny tome.
Bouncing sounds from here to there,
In the shadows, joy's laid bare.

One sings high, another low,
A playful tune, oh what a show!
With each croak, a cheer erupts,
Nature's fun, it just corrupts.

Jumping up without a care,
As a soft breeze tousles hair.
They share their tales with great delight,
And keep the rhythm through the night.

Laughing echoes in the trees,
A chorus for all who might please.
Nature winks while we all sway,
In this whimsical cabaret.

Voices of the Nighttime Grove

In the grove where fun runs wild,
The night is bright, like a child.
Bubbles of laughter fill the air,
As critters leap without a care.

From the pond, a raucous cheer,
Join the gang, come lend your ear!
With every ribbit, jump and skip,
You'll find joy in every quip.

They play hide and seek in the dark,
With a playful leap and a lark.
Whispers rustle through the trees,
As giggles dance upon the breeze.

As shadows sway and friendship glows,
A secret world that only knows.
The night is young, and full of cheer,
In this playful atmosphere.

Synchronized Songs of the Evening

Evening settles, the stage is set,
Nature's choir is a sure bet.
Huddled close, they start to hum,
A funny tune, oh what a drum!

With leaps and bounds, they take a turn,
In a dance of twists, we laugh and yearn.
Hopping here, and skipping there,
Joyful jesters everywhere!

Each note a giggle, each croak a shout,
Who knew the night could bring about?
With playful chirps, they tell their tales,
While the moon grins at their gales.

So as the stars twinkle high above,
Let's join this joyful push and shove.
In perfect sync, they sing their glee,
A nighttime revelry, wild and free!

Dusk's Enchanted Reverie

In the garden, laughter flits,
While shadows dance, and twilight sits.
A symphony of tiny chirps,
As moonlight weaves through fuzzy burps.

The air is thick with silly song,
Where critters bounce, and night plays on.
They jig and jive, a merry show,
Who knew such sounds could steal the glow?

A hopping troupe takes center stage,
In silly hats, they earn their wage.
Each ribbit joined the giggling spree,
As stars above wink joyfully.

Underneath a weeping tree,
The night reveals its jubilee.
With every croak and playful pun,
The endless fun has just begun.

An Anthology of Nighttime Sounds

A chorus rises with the dusk,
A tickle here, a gusty gust.
The garden buzzes, plays a role,
Where tiny fables come to console.

With hops and jumps, they take their chance,
To join the stars in a wild dance.
A wink, a nod, who could resist?
These quirky sounds, they can't be missed!

Giggles echo off the trees,
As whispers roam with gentle breeze.
A funny bounce, a playful shout,
A lullaby of fun, no doubt!

The night ignites with silly vibes,
A joyful feast that nature bribes.
With every sound, a tale unfolds,
In rhymes of glee, the night beholds.

Whispers of Twilight

As daylight fades, a ruckus brews,
In shadows cast, mischief ensues.
With chirpy chirps and bouncy moves,
The night is ripe for crazy grooves.

In secret spots where giggles dwell,
A jumbled tune begins to swell.
Tiny pals unite in jest,
A hootenanny, nature's fest!

The cricket claps and jauntily darts,
Each note a splash in nighttime arts.
With voices high and antics sly,
The evening twists beneath the sky.

A flutter here, a chuckle there,
In every nook, joy fills the air.
Join the parade of frolic and fun,
Under the spell of moonlit run.

Serenade of the Night

As stars peek down with cheeky grins,
The night begins with wild spins.
Under the moon's watchful flare,
Fables rise on the warm night air.

With rhythms light, they play their game,
Each playful sound, a spark of fame.
A croaky laugh, a jumpy cheer,
In this wacky realm, nothing is near.

The garden stirs, a lively gig,
With each little hop, a new twig.
A medley of fun fills the night,
In harmony, no critter takes flight.

So sit and gaze at the bustling scene,
Where silly beings reign supreme.
With every note, a jest we hear,
In the nighttime's song, laughter draws near.

Amphibian Echoes

In the night, they squeak and squeal,
With a chorus that's quite surreal.
Jumping high with such great cheer,
Their little tunes bring us near.

Under the moon, they take their stand,
Making music, oh so grand.
With silly hops and wiggly ways,
They serenade through starlit bays.

Bouncing in rhythm, one by one,
Wobbling like they've just begun.
Each note a giggle, a clumsy dance,
In the breeze, they take their chance.

Who knew such sounds could bring us glee,
From nature's stage, so carefree?
With every chirp, a laugh is shared,
On this stage, we're all prepared.

Duets from the Meadow

In the grass, a duet plays,
With wobbly notes that start to raise.
Their quirky tunes make us smile,
Let's gather 'round and stay a while.

Each note bounces, each trill's a joke,
As they perform, we might just choke.
With a comedy of hops and skips,
Their silly antics give us quips.

They swap the lead, they share the rhyme,
With every leap, they dance in time.
So join this laugh-filled, grassy spree,
Where joy leaps high and spirits are free.

Listen closely, the giggles grow,
A harmony that steals the show.
In the meadow, fun's the rule,
With every croak, we're back in school.

Harmonies Beneath the Stars

Under twinkling lights, they jest,
Piping tunes that are the best.
With mischief woven in their sound,
Each giggle makes the night profound.

In the dark, their laughter rings,
With silly jumps and jiggly flings.
Like a band that's lost their way,
They boast their charms in a natural display.

They hop and shift, a comical show,
With every pause, their antics grow.
Singing songs of joy and fun,
In this concert, we are all won.

Between the leaves, they take their stance,
With nature's giggles, we join the dance.
As stars twinkle, the night does spin,
With melodies that draw us in.

Croaks and Cadences

In the marsh, a rhythm sticks,
With sound effects and plenty of tricks.
Jumping high with a wobbly flair,
Echoes of joy flutter through the air.

They chirp and chortle in silly ways,
Performing antics on muddy bays.
Like comedians on a wet, green stage,
Their funny quirks never age.

With each croak, a funny tale,
Creating laughter without fail.
In this swampy, muddy hold,
Are stories of joy yet to be told.

So gather 'round, enjoy the tune,
As night unfolds under the moon.
With every note, a chuckle or two,
Nature's humor shines right through.

Nature's Whispered Conversations

Under moonlight, the grass does sway,
Tiny voices have much to say.
A chirp here, a croak there, loud and bright,
Nature's gossip keeps us up at night.

In the reeds, they share their tales,
Of awkward jumps and wobbly trails.
A bet on who can leap the farthest,
But tales of splashes are just the hardest!

With twinkling stars to set the stage,
They laugh and scribble jokes on a page.
One claims to dance like a pro on show,
While the others just roll their eyes and go.

Every evening brings a brand new play,
As performers gather in a grand display.
A chorus of chuckles rises from the ground,
In a symphony of jest, joy abounds.

Ballads from the Grassy Reeds

In the hush of twilight, bobbing heads appear,
They share their ballads, oh so queer.
A tune of hops and crazy spins,
As wiggle contests spark a bunch of grins.

Beneath the stars where the tall grass waves,
Their evening antics set up quite the raves.
'Last one to splash is a pickle for sure!'
Is it a rule or a joke? They can't tell for sure.

One claims to croak like the king of a hive,
While others tease, 'More like a fish out of five!'
But laughter erupts with each little blunder,
As their jokes fly high like joyous thunder.

A serenade drifts on the cooling air,
With humorous notes that lead to a dare.
For the boldest of leapfrogs take to the stream,
While the others stay put, living the dream.

Soundtrack of the Shadowy Glade

At dusk's soft fall, the knaves all arrive,
On leafy stages, they truly thrive.
A banter of croaks makes the evening glow,
As if each chuckle was part of the show.

'That jump was epic!' one loudly declares,
While another just stumbles and wipes out with flair.
The air fills with giggles and bold, funny tales,
As they recount travels with clumsy trails.

In the flickering dark, a light in their eyes,
Each ribbit or squeak is a clever disguise.
For beneath every joke lies a tale so sweet,
Of mischief and mayhem, none can defeat.

Around the old pond, they'll gather and share,
With scrumptious humor floating everywhere.
In this soundtrack, pure joy does reside,
A chorus of chuckles that's hard to hide.

Echoes in the Evening Air

As twilight beckons, the night comes alive,
With echoes and laughter, they start to thrive.
A meeting of voices, a whimsical crowd,
In the secrets of dusk, each one feeling proud.

Jests about landings, oops and ohs,
Bringing up memories like rows of rows.
Who can bounce high? Oh, what a sight,
They spin their own yarns under stars shining bright.

One wise old sage hops with grace and glee,
While others remark, 'You've got to see me!'
In this theater of whispers and nightly schemes,
They find all the fun in their froggy dreams.

As the dusk deepens, the antics shift,
New stories emerge with a playful lift.
A legacy sweetened by laughter and cheer,
In the echoes of evening, friendships grow near.

Hidden Melodies of the Wetlands

In the marsh, a commotion, a jump and a croak,
Chirps and sharp banter, oh, what a joke!
A chorus of giggles, they seem to confide,
In a dance of mischief, where secrets reside.

Buzzy-winged gossip spreads fast like a breeze,
While toads swap their tales, dripping with cheese.
They tickle the night with their whimsical sound,
As they leap and they tumble, all merry and round.

Amidst blades of grass, there's a whirl and a twist,
Each note a reminder, of what can't be missed.
With spirals of laughter that echo so wide,
They know how to find joy, nowhere to hide.

A uh-oh up there, something's caught in the reeds,
"It's lunch!" says a froggy, "Let's nibble on seeds!"
The audience crackles, in stitches, they fall,
This fanciful symphony, oh, isn't it all!

The Harmony of Hidden Musicians

Underneath the moonlight, a ruckus unfolds,
Whispers of nonsense, as the night's tale is told.
With a flick and a flap, they plunge into play,
As shadows compose a grand cabaret.

The pluck of a string, a thud and a splash,
Echoes of laughter, both wild and brash.
Each note brings a chuckle, a whoopee or roar,
As the stars join the fun, they're counting to four.

Hidden goodies rustle in the soft, gentle din,
Dodging those curious who try to sneak in.
"Don't peek!" is the shout, then silence ensues,
As the midnight performance gives hints of the blues.

With a flip-flop and tailspin, a dance so sweet,
They tumble and twirl in their nonsensical beat.
An orchestra gathered, both silly and spry,
They welcome the dawn, with a gleam in each eye.

Ribbiting Rhythms Under the Moon

In the glow of the silver, they gather in throngs,
Unleashing their snippets, their silly little songs.
With a bling of the night, they join in the jest,
Add a hop or a skip, they know how to fest!

A toad with a trumpet, so brash and so bold,
Plays jazzy renditions, the stories unfold.
A shy little peeper, just finding its beat,
Joins in for the fun, a comedic retreat.

From willow to pond, they carry the cheer,
While giggles from cattails echo quite near.
With folly and giggle, they dance in the light,
Turning nighttime nonsense to absolute delight.

As the dark starts to soften, the rhythm won't cease,
These merry musicians, they dance to the peace.
With a wink and a grin, they bid the night bye,
"We'll return with the sun," they all shout with a sigh!

Lullabies in the Leafy Hideaway

Nestled in branches, a chorus takes flight,
With whispers of giggles, they welcome the night.
Tiny voices tickle the cool evening air,
As they spin little tales without any care.

The leaves sway and shimmy, they wiggle with glee,
While little toes tap on a soft carpet free.
In this leafy retreat, where moonbeams cascade,
Every hop has a purpose, no need for charade.

What's that in the thicket? A wiggle, a flop!
"Guess who?" they all taunt, "But no one will stop!"
The laughter erupts in a playful tableau,
As shadows entwine in a whimsical show.

With a hum and a burble, they slip into dreams,
Drifting on laughter, or so it seems.
In this hidden abode, where mischief is found,
They drift off, united, with joy all around.

Moonlit Duets on the Marsh's Edge

In shadows they bounce, free and spry,
With long legs, they leap, oh my!
A splash here, a croak there, what a sight,
Nature's silly dance, under moonlight.

With winks and twitching, they take to flight,
Jokes passed along in the still of night.
These comedic creatures, in harmony speak,
Whispers of laughter, oh what a sneak!

They gather around, on a stage so green,
With costumes of mud, they're quite the scene.
A ribbit, a chirp, a jest to share,
Filling the night with musical flair.

When shadows grow long, they scatter and flee,
But not without leaving a giggly spree.
These merry makers, in twilight's embrace,
Leave echoes of joy, a whimsical place.

Echoes of the Dusk Serenade

As twilight falls, the night awakens,
Chirpy little hearts, laughter is taken.
In patches of gloom, adventures unfold,
Tales of the brave, quietly bold.

A chorus of chuckles, from marshland throngs,
In playful sonnets, where everyone belongs.
With leaps and bounds, the jesters glide,
Riding the breezes, they shift with pride.

They croon to the stars, with rhythm absurd,
Creating a symphony, undeterred.
Notes full of mischief, just for the fun,
When dusk bids farewell, their work's never done.

As echoes recede, their laughter remains,
In the heart of the night, their joy sustains.
With each little sound, a story is spun,
In the theater of twilight, their beats are won.

The Unseen Performers of the Night

Behind leaf and log, mischief does dwell,
With little green whispers, they cast their spell.
Proteges of giggles, they hide and sneak,
In the cover of night, it's laughter they seek.

With crinkled wings, they flit and they glide,
In puddle observations, they take such pride.
One hops over here, while two sing a tune,
In the midnight stage, beneath silvered moon.

Their antics unfold, while the stars take a peek,
Pooling of chortles, the brave and the meek.
Rehearsed in the silence, their charm flows free,
Whipping up rhythms of joyful decree.

Each leap is a giggle, each turn is a cheer,
They banish the shadows, with spirits so clear.
Unseen but so present, these jesters portray,
The essence of mirth in the night's ballet.

Rhythms in the Stillness of Twilight

In the hush of dusk, where the stillness drapes,
Silly chums gather, all dressed in capes.
With sounds like popcorn, they bounce with glee,
Creating a ballet, so wild and free.

They twirl on the stage of nature's grand floor,
In moonbeam spotlight, they never bore.
A hiccup, a quack, a squeal from the reeds,
The clowns of the marsh, doing funny deeds.

Joking and jiving, with each little hop,
Wonders abound as they never stop.
A tap on the water, a rustle of grass,
Comedy unfolds as the moments pass.

So let's raise a cheer for the night's fab troupe,
With chorus and giggles, the air's one big loop.
As they serenade twilight from dusk to day,
These merry night jesters surely steal the play.

The Nocturnal Chorus

In the garden, the night awakens,
Sounds of chirps, no one is fakin'.
A serenade of silly beats,
Wiggly dancers on tiny feet.

With a hop and a jump, they play,
Who knew night brought such ballet?
Bouncing here, then over there,
All while pretending they don't care.

Tiny musicians in deep green,
Performing antics, oh so clean.
Each note a giggle, each pause a tease,
Nature's jesters, if you please.

As stars wink and the moonlight beams,
They frolic on, fulfilling dreams.
With each silly sound, they shine bright,
This madness brings delight tonight!

Murmurs in the Moonlight

Under a sky so wide and vast,
Chirps and croaks, a blast from the past!
Echoes of laughter in the still air,
Join the fun, if you dare.

In the pond, a splash and a splish,
Making merry with every swish.
The night is alive with giggly quips,
As they sway and twist with tipsy flips.

A raucous symphony takes the stage,
What a funny, silly age!
When the moon giggles back in light,
It adds to the joy of this wild night.

So come one, come all, to this fun fair,
Lively sounds mingle thick in the air.
As whispers turn into fits of laughter,
Nature's show, happily ever after!

Twilight Duos

As daylight dips and shadows grow,
Duets of nature steal the show.
A croaky voice, a chirpy tweet,
Creating rhythms on small, swift feet.

One near the stream, another with flair,
Jumping and singing without a care.
In a breezy waltz, they take their chance,
Spinning and twirling in a silly dance.

With bubbles rise from below the hues,
Each pair grins in classic views.
They laugh at stars up in the dome,
This is truly their lotus bloom.

Merriment rises with every croon,
Underneath the watchful moon.
Each sound a jest, each pause a jest,
These twilight duos are simply the best!

Songs from the Waterside

Beside the pond where shadows glide,
A playful chorus can't be denied.
Silly harmonies, what a delight,
As laughter carries into the night.

Each rustle and ripple sets the tone,
Tomorrow's tales will be well-known.
What antics await in the light of day?
For now, it's simply time to play.

With giddy hops and cheeky grins,
They clamor through the water's spins.
Swaying low, touching the ground,
All while making a silly sound.

So gather 'round for the night's delight,
For joy dances here, oh what a sight!
In the laughter of weeks that soar,
Songs from the waterside call for more!

Melodic Meanderings

Tiny dancers hidden away,
Under the moonlight, they play.
Jumping and leaping in merry tune,
Counting stars, a silly boon.

With the night air all alive,
Bouncing legs, they twist and thrive.
They croak out jokes, their favorite fare,
It's comedy hour, do you dare?

Shadows jump with each wild note,
Silly songs make all hearts float.
They chirp and chuckle, a raucous choir,
A giggling ball that lifts us higher.

Under the splash of silver light,
Chuckling critters spark delight.
Hop and skip, what a funny sight,
Singing silly songs through the night.

Euphony of the Evening

In the gloom, the giggles rise,
As little voices harmonize.
Ribbits blend with howls and chats,
An orchestra of chuckling sprats.

With each leap, a laugh resounds,
Through the reeds, the cackle bounds.
They trade tall tales, oaths, and pranks,
In playful banter, silence sinks.

As the moon hangs like a gift,
Parody strolls with a little lift.
The harmony dances out of sight,
Compose a jingle under the starlight.

Nature's jesters take the stage,
Giggling softly, they engage.
Listen close to their fun parade,
Nighttime's jests, joyfully laid.

Nature's Symphony

From the brush, a chorus spills,
Frothy laughter, effortless thrills.
Little friends in quirky lines,
Creating jams with silly signs.

Toadstool hats and croaky grins,
Jumping jests like they're all twins.
Quips and quotes fly through the breeze,
Riddles popping 'neath the trees.

They jest above a rippling stream,
Each croak steals the center beam.
Slapstick humor, a leafy play,
Rolling laughter 'till break of day.

In this void, a playful throng,
Cheering echoes, evergreen song.
Hop along, don't miss the beat,
Nature's fun can't be beat!

Chants of the Marshland

In the marsh, where giggles stir,
Each waddle, hop, a joyful blur.
Fuzzy faces, brief debates,
Over who leaps best, at what rates.

Every splash serves up a joke,
An amphibian's playful poke.
Chattering glee in moonlit pools,
Ambushing stillness, breaking tools.

Wetland antics, pranks galore,
Every croak shouts out for more.
In a jesting whirl, they twirl around,
Mausoleum of laughter sound.

As shadows dance and mischief blooms,
They craft their tunes in nature's rooms.
In the marsh, where giggles say,
Life is best in a funny way.

Rustic Reflections

In shadows cast by moonlit beams,
The garden hums with silly schemes.
A chorus sings of summer's cheer,
While buzzing pals shout, "We're all here!"

With tiny leaps and flopping feet,
They hold a dance, oh, what a feat!
A patchwork quilt of croaks and chirps,
In harmony, their laughter burps!

The evening air, a teasing breeze,
Unruly antics beneath the trees.
With every hop, a new surprise,
In the night's giggle, joy will rise.

Each creature dons a playful mask,
In this wild show, they dare to bask.
Glimmers of mischief in their eyes,
As they twist and turn beneath the skies.

Chants of the Inhabitants

Upon the bank, the ruckus swells,
With cheerful tricks and echoed yells.
A symphony of funny sights,
As laughter dances through the nights.

A jester leans on a slippery ledge,
With a thump and a splash, he makes his pledge:
To jump so high and land so low,
The audience roars at the daring show!

With tiny tails and bulging eyes,
They share their stories; each a prize.
A bumpy road of bounces bright,
In the quirkiest stories told tonight.

As silliness rules this shady grove,
They leap and laugh; oh, how they rove!
In the orchestra of goofy glee,
Each note a tickle, wild and free.

Interludes of the Wild

In the twilight, frolic and fawn,
A ribbit here and a croak at dawn.
With silly giggles, they play on grass,
A jolly tease as the moments pass.

Squishy mud and muddy feet,
A slip, a trip, what a chewy treat!
In timeless jests, they rediscover,
That play's the perfect way to hover!

Chasing shadows, creating seams,
Twisting tales like giddy dreams.
Oh, the sights that laughter brings,
In jumbles of joy, their spirit sings.

So gather round, in evening's light,
With winks and nods, they hold on tight.
For every bounce, a tale is spun,
In this wild dance, they're having fun!

Symphony of the Sedge

In the hush where the waters flow,
A riot of sound begins to grow.
Jumpy fellows with a twist of fate,
Blend their voices, the wild create.

Beneath the stars, they hum in tune,
Each croak and chirp a jovial boon.
With every leap, their antics rise,
The evening quacks and laughter flies!

As gales sweep through, they shimmy and sway,
In muddy puddles, they dance and play.
With hops and wheezes, they make a scene,
A frolicsome ball, a nighttime dream.

In the orchestra of the night, they sing,
A merry tune, let the joy take wing.
With playful hearts, beneath the moon's gleam,
In raucous revelry, life is a dream.

Whispering Tales of the Wetlands

In the mud where creatures sing,
A chorus of legs hops on a spring.
Lily pads wear goofy hats,
While all around swirl silly spats.

With every splash, a giggle grows,
A tiny kingfisher's dance, who knows?
The rushes sway, they laugh in glee,
As bobbing bugs sing out in spree.

A turtle yawns, sprawled on a log,
Turning dreams to mist with a fog.
Even the reeds seem to sway in jest,
As night-time antics put fun to the test.

Hidden chuckles beneath the moon,
A tale of jumps in rhythmic tune.
Each croak and chirp tells something absurd,
In this lush land, funny sounds are heard.

Melodious Shadows of the Night

Underneath the sleepy skies,
A party meets with winking eyes.
Bouncing buddies, feeling spry,
Trading jokes as night slips by.

Moonlight dips in playful glee,
Where late-night snacks hang from a tree.
One slips on a dew-kissed leaf,
The laughter echoes, no sign of grief.

A dance-off starts, who takes the crown?
With wobbly legs, they all fall down.
Just when the night seems calm and tame,
A ripple of giggles fans the flame.

In the shadows, friendships grow,
While silly shadows dance to and fro.
A funny world beyond what's known,
As melodies of laughter are overthrown.

Nature's Cacophony Under a Blanket of Stars

Stars wink above the raucous spree,
While rustling leaves hum happily.
An army of chirps fills the air,
With giggles and snorts that hang with flair.

Each creature struts in their own way,
In a symphony where all may play.
An echoing laugh from a turtle shy,
Who nearly took flight but forgot how to fly.

Laughter spills across the swampy floor,
With one brave soul who roars with lore.
In every nook, they're making noise,
Together they bring the night such joys.

Though chaos reigns under celestial lights,
Jokes bouncing high like daring flights.
In this wild world, take off your shoes,
You'll hear their tales of humorous blues.

The Symphonic Glade's Secret

In a glade where giggles play,
The music stirs both night and day.
With a push and pull, the breezes sway,
Tickling secrets that dare to stray.

A band of misfits, bright and bold,
Share mysteries within tales told.
With cleverly crafted leaps and bounds,
They frolic beneath the silent sounds.

A frog in glasses leads the song,
While laughter ripples all along.
With notes of joy in a bouncy heap,
They weave their stories, no need for sleep.

In harmony, they find a way,
To spin and dance and brightly play.
So come and join this merry jam,
In the glade's heart, chaos is never bland.

Cadences in the Quiet

In night's soft giggles, they plot with ease,
Jumping and chirping under moonlit trees.
A comedy troupe in the dark they play,
With tiny high notes and a loud Cabaret.

They hide in the grasses, just under the stars,
Telling their tales of mischief from afar.
With every odd hop and their musical flair,
They'll have you in stitches — but who's really there?

With tiny green legs and a raucous delight,
They dance through the shadows, a silly sight.
A performance so rich, you can't help but grin,
As each little actor hops right back in.

At dawn they'll retreat, their antics all done,
In silence they vanish, the night was such fun.
With echoes remaining, a memory sweet,
Of laughs in the dark and their rough-and-tumble beat.

Echoing Dreams

In the still of the night, there's a thing that occurs,
A symphony plays, though no one quite stirs.
It starts with a croak, then a squeak joins the fun,
Each note gets a laugh, till the moon says it's done.

The tiniest jesters make quite a loud show,
Ribbiting jokes in a head-to-toe flow.
Each line they emit is a burst of delight,
Leaving giggles and chuckles in thick, starry night.

Who knew that this gathering was all such a jest?
With hops and with hoots, they evict every stress.
The chorus gets louder, as they know what to do,
Their laughter contagious, it's catching for you!

So, listen a moment, let laughter unfold,
To the whimsical rhymes that the night has retold.
With dreams made of humor, sleep tight, don't you fret,
For tomorrow at dusk, there's more joy to be met.

Songs of the Serene

In gardens where whispers twirl and they spin,
A band strikes a chord, where adventure begins.
With hops by the flowers and skips through the reeds,
Nature's own jesters fulfill all our needs.

The players in green take their turn in the light,
With verses of fun that dance through the night.
They hum and they buzz, with a grin on each face,
As laughter erupts in this musical place.

Each jump holds a pun, each chirp holds a jest,
An improvised giggle, a hope for the best.
What whimsy is born from such jovial ties,
Each lyric a jest that brings tears to our eyes.

So let the songs carry on through the breeze,
While hearts fill with laughter, let's bask in the tease.
For the night is a canvas, with humor it gleams,
Painting pictures of joy from our echoing dreams.

Melodies of the Meadow

In the bright of the field, they gather with grace,
Stirring up symphonies in this wide-open space.
With wind in their wings, and a laugh in each croak,
A green medley forms, in a joyous cloak.

They leap and they squeak, with a touch of the quirky,
While melodies tumble, all snappy and jerky.
A tap dance of notes in the soft, setting sun,
With each giggle shared, there's found endless fun.

Their chirps turn to jests, as the sun dips away,
Each sound a reminder of night's bright ballet.
In laughter, they flourish, as stars slowly peek,
With tunes that could heal even hearts that are weak.

So come join the revel, in the meadow of cheer,
Where every small giggle brings kind spirits near.
With joy colored bright, in the laughter so clear,
Let's dance with the shadows till morning draws near.

A Pair of voices in the Dim Light

In the dusk, two pals croon,
With chirps and hops, they start soon.
A comical tune, oh what a sight,
As shadows dance in the soft moonlight.

One on a log, the other in grass,
Who knew this night could be such a blast?
Their laughter echoes, an odd little sound,
While critters gather, all around.

With winks and giggles, they play their game,
Not a care in the world, not a hint of shame.
In their small world, joy is the theme,
And each note brings a silly dream.

So chuckle along, let the night unfold,
In the dim light, stories are told.
A whimsical night, a vibrant affair,
With two jolly souls, floating in air.

Celestial Chants from the Meadow

Beneath bright stars, a tune does rise,
Harmonious laughter fills the skies.
With tiny hops and silly jumps,
The pitter-patter is music's thumps.

In patches green, they sway and twirl,
Each note a giggle, a playful whirl.
Two mischief-makers, under the moon,
Their merry sounds—a perfect tune.

They jive and jolt till the dawn does break,
Not a thought of rest, for fun's at stake.
With whispers and chuckles, they play their part,
A sing-along symphony straight from the heart.

So dance with abandon, let worries fly,
Under starlit skies, they reach for the sky.
With every chorus, the universe sways,
In this meadow of laughter, where joy always stays.

Treetop Melodies and Swampy Harmonies

Up in the branches, the joyful jive,
Swaying along, where the critters thrive.
Their silly songs echo through the air,
In a concert hall that has no care.

Down by the bog, it's a splashy parade,
Waddling and wiggling, they serenade.
A raucous mix, both high and low,
Creating a show, just for the glow.

Mirth and mayhem, a grand ol' time,
With each plucky note, they strike the chime.
In every whisk and wiggle, there's laughter galore,
As nature's chorus cries out for more.

From treetops to wetlands, the humor abounds,
In a whimsical world of delight that surrounds.
So let us join in this musical spree,
With glee and giggles, wild and free.

Nightfall's Rhythmic Conversation

As the day takes a bow, night takes its cue,
Two rascals converse, with antics anew.
Their banter a puzzle—a riddle, a joke,
In the softened hush where the twilight awoke.

Bouncing on pebbles, a rhythmic delight,
They tap out their tales, so carefree and bright.
With flashes of wisdom, wrapped in jest,
Each story told makes their hearts feel blessed.

Flooded with laughter, the warm evening glows,
As the moon winks down, and mischief flows.
In the comedy of nature, they play their role,
With a wink here and there, they lighten the soul.

From dusk till dawn, let the giggles resound,
In this odd rendezvous, joy is unbound.
With hearts full of laughter, faces aglow,
Their nighttime concert is quite the show.

Evening's Lullaby

When shadows stretch and giggles soar,
The orchestra begins, what fun is in store!
A chirp here, a croak there, all in a row,
Who knew bedtime could put on such a show!

With tiny feet tapping a silly dance,
They hop and they skip, oh, look at them prance!
A serenade's brewing, just watch and behold,
As laughter and music together unfold!

The moon takes its seat, all ready to glow,
While stars cast their wishes, putting on a show.
This nighttime parade, it's sure to delight,
With creatures amusing beneath the moonlight!

As night draws its curtain, the sound softly swells,
With giggles and glimmers from nature's own bells.
A whimsical ending, a slip and a slide,
In this lullaby dance, let yourself take a ride!

Rhythms of the Forest

In the heart of the woods, a ruckus begins,
As small voices shout, and laughter spins.
A cast of comical critters all cheer,
Adding joy to the evening, our favorite time of year!

Leaves rustle softly, they join in the fun,
With a boom and a bop, oh, how they run!
The beat keeps on bouncing, in rhythm they sway,
A whimsical dance, to end the day!

Dressed in mismatched outfits, oh what a sight,
Each jump and jive brings sheer delight.
A solo on leaves, a duet on a stone,
This jig in the dark makes you feel right at home!

And as the sun dips, the concert completes,
With chuckles and cheers, not one soul retreats.
In the rhythm of laughter, mischief takes flight,
A joyful soirée, till the morning light!

Melodies of Dusk

As twilight arrives with a wink and a teasing,
The melody starts, you can hear the sneezing!
A chorus of quirks fills the dusky air,
Each note a strange giggle, a laugh to share.

Bouncing on twigs, the sound takes a leap,
In the thick of the grass, where giggles creep.
The night opens up, like a book left to read,
With every new chuckle, more smiles we need!

With shadows at play, they form a parade,
Under twinkling lights, oh, the laughter won't fade!
An encore of chuckles, a symphony sweet,
Dance to these tunes on your wiggly feet!

In the fading light, let the fun slip and slide,
With melodies ringing, let silliness guide.
As dusk turns to night, keep your spirits high,
In this funny ensemble, together we'll fly!

Nature's Ballad

In a meadow alive with a curious tune,
Creatures convene, oh how they can croon!
With hops that are bouncy, and twirls that amaze,
Nature's own cast puts on silly plays.

Under the spotlight of the shimmering stars,
The laughter erupts, oh who took the cars?
Each twinkle a wink, each rustle a jest,
With cheerleaders cheering, they're truly the best!

As laughter emanates from bushes and trees,
A duet in the darkness, a tickle in the breeze.
The fun unravels like a magical thread,
With jokes and with pranks, no reason for dread!

So listen closely, as night wraps its cloak,
The humor of nature, let's revel and poke.
With giggles and grins, immerse in the thrill,
In this playful ballad, there's magic to spill!

Duality of the Wild

One hops with flair, a jump so tall,
The other sings sweet, a croak to enthrall.
They trade silly tales, under moonlight bright,
In a world that's alive, with laughter and light.

A dance on the leaf, a twirl on the ground,
The rhythm of nature, in giggles resound.
Wings and webs weave a story so fine,
Where the oddest pairs blend with the divine.

In puddles they splash, in wild delight,
Creating a show, under stars shining bright.
With raucous applause, their antics ensue,
As the night wears on, and the skies turn blue.

Oh what a jest, in this droll charade,
Where every odd friend has a role to parade.
In the quiet of woods, joy bids them to play,
For laughs echo here, keeping worries at bay.

Serenades of the Swamp

A muddy ballet, with leaps and hip hops,
Two jesters take lead, while the moon briefly stops.
With bug-eyed bravado, they croon a sweet song,
Each note full of whimsy, where all else belongs.

With spontaneity bursting, they frolic with glee,
Mixing up rhythms as wild as can be.
On lily pads perched, they strike up a tune,
Singing the night back, under the swoon of the moon.

A punchline delivered with each little ribbit,
Where audience giggles take shape as they quibbit.
In the heart of the dusk, no worries can stay,
As melody swirls in enchanting display.

When dawn draws near, and the laughter subsides,
They chuckle at dreams where the magic abides.
With snickers and glances, their friendships remain,
In the swamp of the night, joy dances like rain.

Voices in the Shadows

In the hushed twilight, a riddle unfolds,
Two voices emerge, mischievous yet bold.
With chirps and with chuckles, they paint the night sky,
In a game of wits, none would dare to deny.

With shadows as blankets, they plan their next jest,
Hiding in clumps, where the bravest still rest.
One whispers a secret, with grins ear to ear,
As chuckles and giggles dance close to one's ear.

A banquet of wit, they feast on pure glee,
With shadows for company, and laughs like the sea.
Each jest is a jewel, a sparkling delight,
In the chorus of chaos, under cover of night.

But oh, what awaits in the break of the day?
A flicker of panic, then swiftly they sway.
With camaraderie brimming, and humor ablaze,
Together they plot for the next night's malaise.

Dance of the Night Creatures

When the sky drapes black, come the jigs and the jiggles,
With shimmies and shakes, turning silence to giggles.
Upon twinkling grass and the cool, soothing breeze,
Two pals make a splash, where laughter's at ease.

With hops like confetti, they twirl round and round,
Each frolic a jest, every shiver profound.
In the chaos of merriment, joy spills from their mouths,
Drawing sights and sounds from the faraway south.

A symphony echoes with every odd stance,
With snickers and howls, they invite you to dance.
The crunch of the night air, the glow of the stars,
Where misfits and rhythms spin tales from afar.

As dawn peeks behind, with its soft-colored blush,
The spectacle fades in the morning's light hush.
Still echoes of laughter, in the hearts they will stay,
For the dance of the night is a comedic ballet.

Night Whispers in the Marsh

In the dark where shadows play,
The night creatures start to sway.
A leggy lad with a crazy hop,
Who laughs aloud and can't be stopped.

With little friends they form a band,
They crack jokes about the land.
A chorus of chuckles fills the air,
As moonlit beams dance everywhere.

A slow waltz across the bog,
A wiggle here from a silly frog.
They trade silly jests with glee,
In this wild, yet funny spree.

With nimble feet and splashes wide,
They leap about with froggy pride.
The night is filled with jovial cheer,
As laughter echoes far and near.

Lyric Echoes from the Pond

In the murk of twilight glow,
A quack and ribbit steal the show.
With splashes small and bubbles round,
Who knew such fun could so abound?

Glimmers of mischief in their eyes,
As rippling waves bring comic sighs.
Two pals with jokes of croaks and spins,
They play all night; the laughter wins.

A limerick sung atop a log,
With a wink from a chummy frog.
Their antics make the night surreal,
As grins grow wide with every squeal.

When moonlight glimmers all about,
It's time for tunes without a doubt.
They'll serenade the night unfurled,
With whimsical sounds that share their world.

Serenade of the Twilight Singers

When the sun sinks low and shadows rise,
The evening crooners start to improvise.
A jig and jive with every croak,
Together they giggle, all in good poke.

Lively notes fill the dampened air,
With playful banter and little care.
Each jest a tune, each poke a rhyme,
Creating a symphony, lost in time.

With antics fresh and stories spun,
They laugh and sing, their night's begun.
Dancing on pads, in an amusing race,
Ribbit and chuckles in every space.

In the stillness, friendships ring,
A spark of joy in everything.
As nature sways to their vibrant song,
Their romp through the night feels oh-so-long.

Duets Beneath the Stars

As the starlight begins to peek,
A duet starts with play and cheek.
One hops high, the other spins,
In this merry world where laughter wins.

With every note, a splash of fun,
They take their turns, not just one.
A croaky tale, a funny tale,
As silhouettes beneath the veil.

A jestful nudge and playful cheer,
Each flick of tongue brings all near.
With glimmering eyes, they share their part,
Leaving the night with a ticklish heart.

In the tapestry of shimmering light,
Their frolic ripples through the night.
Two jesters in a whimsical play,
Under a sky of stars at bay.

Echoes Through the Canopy

In the moonlight's gleam, they sing their tune,
Jumping high, under the silver moon.
With a ribbit and a laughter, they start their dance,
Making shadows move; it's a froggy romance.

Leaves sway gently to their merry song,
As if nature's joined in, where we all belong.
A playful croak here, a little chirp there,
Echoes of joy float lightly in the air.

What's that sound? A little buzz from the ground,
Mismatched duets make a funny round.
These little creatures, a comical crew,
Swaying and playing, oh, what a view!

The night gets on, the fun never ends,
As laughter and croaking become best of friends.
Under the starlight, they leap and play,
Who knew nature had such funny ballet?

Whimsical Whispers

In the garden's glow, they craft their tales,
Jumping on leaves, wearing leaf-like veils.
With sounds of joy, they liven the night,
Creating a ruckus, such a silly sight!

Pitter-patter paws, flapping little wings,
A chorus so lively, oh, the joy it brings!
With each little note, they tease the breeze,
A melody of mischief among the trees.

Oh, listen close, can you hear the fuss?
A choir of laughter in nature's bus!
As shadows dance and twirl in delight,
They stage a show, under the moonlight.

Every croak a pun, every hop a jest,
In this midnight circus, they've got the best!
With a twinkle of eyes, they wink and cheer,
Join this frolic, their family is here!

Harmonies of the Hidden

In the tall grass, a clever tune,
Sings of fun beneath the moon.
A tap, a clap, a jolly jump,
In the night's embrace, they cavort and thump.

With a flip and a flop, they dance so gay,
Creating mishaps in their own ballet.
A splash in the puddle, a squish on the ground,
Laughter erupts, a joyful sound!

Witty whispers float through the air,
As cheeky creatures share a dare.
One leaps high, with a splashy plop,
And everyone giggles; it's a fabulous flop!

Their silly antics fill the night sky,
With a hop and a skip, they leap so high.
Gather 'round friends, let's join the spree,
For these hidden harmonies bring pure glee!

Twilight's Embrace

When twilight falls, they start the show,
With laughter and leaps, to and fro.
A giggle here, a hop so spry,
Beneath the stars, they dance and fly.

In their playful realm, none are shy,
As one tumbles quick, the others sigh,
With a wink, they nod, as if to say,
What a silly game we play all day!

Underneath the sky, where shadows creep,
A jest here, a laugh, a leap and a sweep.
The night is full of cheer and jest,
These merry performers are simply the best!

And though the hour may grow late,
Their antics continue, it's never too straight.
In twilight's embrace, they frolic and prance,
For life's but a joke—a grand, funny dance!

Lullabies from the Pond

In the twilight, croaks collide,
A chorus where the night does hide.
Bubbles pop with every pause,
Nature giggles, just because.

Whispers ride the evening breeze,
Wiggly tails, a tune to tease.
Water splashes in delight,
Lively antics take their flight.

A bouncing ball of plunk and play,
While shadows dance and leap away.
Ripples giggling, puddles gleam,
Though they wish for a more serious theme.

As stars peek out from velvet skies,
Ribbits echo, oh what a surprise!
With every leap, the fun expands,
Joyful echoes from tiny bands.

Rhythmic Revelations

With every plop, a secret shared,
Each little splash, someone prepared.
In the night, they sing their tales,
Of mischief wrapped in murky trails.

Jumping high, then sliding back,
They plot their jumps and plan their track.
The muddy banks are sticky ground,
Where giggles tumble all around.

Every note is sharp and bright,
As critters vie for stage delight.
A fiddler's bow plays on a leaf,
Conducting laughter, oh so brief.

The moon above, a shining eye,
Winks at the chaos, oh my, oh my!
Their rhythm beats, a silly glee,
Nature's pranksters, wild and free.

The Harmony of Dusk

Under the shade of willow's sway,
Jokes are tossed from twirls of play.
A croaky tune, a buzzing hum,
Whimsical vibes where all is fun.

Splashed reflections in heavy air,
Where giggling pals spread joyful flare.
Echoes stretch through leaves above,
Grumpy owls will never shove.

The sky turns pink, a wink in sight,
As laughter twirls in soft twilight.
Chirps and laughs, a light serenade,
In this playful, glimmering parade.

With every plunk, a chuckle shared,
These little jesters, oh so dared.
They flip and flop, then take a bow,
A raucous feast, oh look at them now!

Melodies on the Breezes

Breezy nights where giggles meet,
Tiny feet in quick retreat.
A splash, a croon, a bouncy cheer,
Silly whispers you can hear.

Bouncing balls, that's their sound,
Not a soul is stuck to ground.
Sent to strut beneath the moon,
Their funny pranks a hidden tune.

Dancing shadows, playful prance,
In the swamp, they take their chance.
Echoing laughter swims upstream,
Filling the night with the wildest dream.

Conductor stars in mismatched hats,
Leading all the cheeky chats.
In ponds where creatures twist and play,
Nightly jokes light up the way.

Glistening Nights

In the moon's soft glow, they dance and play,
Legs a-jumpin' in a wild ballet.
Chirpy tunes ripple across the field,
As nature's orchestra refuses to yield.

With a splash and a croak, they join the fun,
Each note a joke beneath the sun.
Bounding about, they leap and prance,
Nature's jesters in a zany dance.

Beneath starry skies, the laughter swells,
In the symphony where mischief dwells.
They tell tall tales in harmonic flow,
Of nights like these, we all should know.

In a gleeful chirp or a giddy sound,
Every critter knows where joy is found.
So grab a seat, come join the night,
With these funny friends, everything's right.

Rustic Rhythms

In the grassy nook, a party brews,
With funny faces, in odd shoes.
They chirp and ribbit, a raucous crew,
Bouncing along, in a whimsical queue.

A banter of hums, a fiddle or two,
Creating a ruckus, as good friends do.
With every hop, a rippling cheer,
In this rustic place, let laughter steer.

They croon tales of picnic blunders,
Of soggy sandwiches and funny wonders.
Around the pond, they spin their lore,
Making you giggle 'til your sides are sore.

So tip your hat to the night's charade,
With this merry bunch in a grand parade.
Together they revel, with joy unconfined,
In rustic rhythms that tickle the mind.

Lyrics of the Land

In a patch of grass, with glee they sing,
Their nonsense verses, a comical fling.
Each hop and croak relays a jest,
Nature's clowns, always dressed best.

Around the pond, with a splash and a cheer,
They spin silly rhymes for all to hear.
No need for scripts, just pure delight,
In melodies woven from day to night.

With every note, there's laughter stuck,
In the air so thick, you can't help but pluck.
They chirrup and croon, a playful team,
In this lyrical land, we all can dream.

So raise your voice to join the playlist,
These jolly singers, you can't resist.
With laughter echoing from every glade,
In the lyrics of the land, joy won't fade.

Silhouettes in Song

In the twilight dim, shadows bounce and sway,
A giggle here, a ribbit there, at play.
With silhouettes dancing on the bright moonbeam,
They craft a tale, a whimsical dream.

A chorus of chuckles,
filling the night,
As joyous mischief takes glorious flight.
With leaps so grand, they glide through the air,
In this playful pageant, smiles to spare.

The crickets' jests and the frogs' playful winks,
In every sharp note, the silliness shrinks.
The night's a stage, a hilarious show,
With every funny quip, the laughter will grow.

So join this parade of giggles and glee,
As shadows unite in absurd jubilee.
For in song's warm embrace, we all belong,
Reveling together, in silhouettes of song.

Twilight's Musical Tale

In the dusk, a chatter starts,
Jumping sounds that split the air.
The band of night croons with playful hearts,
As they dance without a care.

A chorus sings from every nook,
With the rhythm of the night in tow.
Tiny voices form a witty book,
Oh, the antics they bestow!

Their symphony's a silly game,
With notes that tickle every ear.
They laugh and jump, with zest and fame,
Creating mirthful songs, we cheer!

So join the fun, let laughter soar,
For this twilight show's a sight.
With giggles echoing to the core,
These whimsical sounds bring pure delight.

The Realm of Echoes

Down by the pond, the echoes ring,
A croaky treat for all who hear.
Gleeful sounds take flight and swing,
A joyful jest that's crystal clear.

They chat and laugh, no room for gloom,
Each note a whisper, bright and bold.
The night is filled with laughs that bloom,
In tales that never grow old.

With each small leap, a giggle flies,
An upbeat dance on lily pads.
They sing of life and moonlit skies,
Unruly fun, no time for fads!

So come and join this merry throng,
Let happiness lead the way.
In this realm where voices belong,
The night is young, let's laugh and play!

Crooning Under the Stars

Underneath the twinkling lights,
The night brigade begins to croon.
With goofy tunes and silly sights,
Each note shines bright like a balloon.

They hop and skip with glee in sight,
A party where the nicknames flow.
With leaps of joy, they take to flight,
Beneath a silver starry glow.

Each chirp and chuckle paints the air,
A funny song from tiny throats.
As crazy rhythms swirl with flair,
They celebrate in joyful notes!

So let's all join this merry show,
With laughter shared beneath the night.
The silly sounds, we'll let them flow,
As happiness takes its flight!

Living Lyricism

In the moonlight, where the jesters meet,
A lively band begins to play.
With whispers sweet and playful beat,
They twirl and dip in wild ballet.

Each laugh explodes in harmony,
Creating tunes that bounce and swirl.
With mischief in their company,
They revel in a dance unfurl.

The world becomes a stage so grand,
Where funny quirks take center stage.
With every leap, they form a band,
In this jesting, nature's page!

So raise a cheer for sounds so bright,
And let their music fill the air.
For in this night, all feels just right,
Living lyricism everywhere!

www.ingramcontent.com/pod-product-compliance
Lightning Source LLC
Chambersburg PA
CBHW072148200426
43209CB00051B/837